CONCISE COLLECTION

Military Badges and Insignia

Mark Lloyd

Grange BOOKS

Published in 1995
by Grange Books
An imprint of Grange Books Plc.
The Grange
Grange Yard
London SE1 3AG

ISBN 1 85627 792 5

Printed in Italy.

Right: Chinese People's Navy troops

Acknowledgments
The photographs in this book were supplied by the
following photographers and agencies:
Department of Defense front cover, 7, 8, 9, 10, 12, 13;
New Zealand Army 45.
Guy Taylor 6, 30, 31, 32, 34, 35, 38, 41.
TRH Pictures 25; Robin Adshead 19; Yves Debay 23,
26; DoD 4, 14, 28, 42; P Hogan 17; MOD 16; NATO
29; E Nevill 15, 18, 33, 39; John Norris 20; Press
Association 22; Soldier 21, 46; Guy Taylor 37.
All artwork supplied by the Maltings Partnership with
the exception of those on pages 7, 10, 14, 16, 18, 38,
45 and 46 which were supplied by Andrew Wright.

Contents

Introduction

Military badges and insignia are nothing new. As long ago as the 12th and 13th centuries, Crusaders on passage to the Holy Land donned the red cross of Christ in anticipation of future battles with the infidel. Two centuries later, heavily armoured knights bore standards into battle as a simple mode of identity. However, it was not until the 18th century that the mass of ordinary troops began to wear any form of regimental insignia.

By the 1850s, individual soldiers could be recognized by the style and cut of their uniforms and by their often large and ornate hat badges. Cardigan's troopers before the Charge of the Light Brigade wore magnificent – if impractical – tight cherry-coloured trousers and gilded jackets, all purchased at great expense by their commanding officer.

The American Civil War brought about a revolution in the wearing of military insignia. Regionally-formed units were issued initially with uniforms purchased by local subscription. Little if any attention was paid to national or even state dress regulations, so much so that it was not at all unusual for regiments to muster with ten independent companies each dressed entirely differently. As the 'ninety-day' war dragged on into its second and third year, personalized uniforms wore out and were begrudgingly exchanged for blue and grey

state issue. Even so, individual state and county insignia survived, occasionally to the very end of the war. The Pennsylvania Volunteers continued to sport animal tails in the back of their hats, the Iron Brigade of the West their large Hardee hats, and Hood's Texas Brigade their proud lone star.

The far-sighted Cardwell reforms of 1871 saw the revolutionary introduction of the county system into the British Army. Each county regiment recruited within its own geographical confines, researched its traditions and was issued with a cap badge reflecting where possible its historical antecedents.

Twenty-five years later the Boers, excellent marksmen all, taught the world a salutary lesson. It was no longer possible to wear bright uniforms in the face of an enemy armed with rifles capable of hitting their targets at ranges in excess of 1,000 metres. With the exception of France, which clung to its 'pantalons rouges' and its blue patrol jackets, every major army sought the protective anonymity of blue, grey or khaki. Cap badges and shoulder boards, in many instances similar to those worn today, were introduced in an attempt to preserve regimental identity.

As military proficiency improved, so the skill-at-arms and trade badges proliferated. Newly-formed élite units of marines

and paratroopers were issued with distinctive green and maroon berets and accompanying 'wings', especially in World War II. Certain insignia, notably the winged dagger, became synonymous with excellence throughout the world.

Because of the recent rise in terrorism, a number of élite units nowadays only wear their full insignia within the safety of their own barracks. The sand-coloured beret of the British SAS will rarely be seen in the field. Other units, notably the United States's Green Berets and the British Parachute Regiment, continue to wear their berets and distinctive insignia in action, arguing that the very sight of them strikes fear in the hearts of the enemy.

Above: Fallschirmjäger, West Germany

82nd Airborne (All American)

Badge: A shield-shaped 'flash' in the unit colours, worn on a red beret (reintroduced in 1980). Centred on the flash, officers wear metal rank insignia, enlisted men the distinctive unit crest

Specialist Insignia: A red, white and blue divisional patch, comprising the letters AA in a circle within a square, is worn on the left shoulder by all ranks. Parachute qualification wings are worn over the left breast

History: The US Army's 82nd (All American) Airborne Division is one of the

largest airborne formations in the world and crucial to America's strategic combat policy.

Formed as an infantry unit in August 1917, the 82nd was deployed to France where it spent a record number of days at the front. Deactivated in 1919, the 82nd Division was reconstituted as an airborne formation in 1942 and distinguished itself in action throughout World War II. By June 1945 the Division had spent nearly two years abroad, including 442 days in combat. Since then the 82nd Airborne Division has been in combat a further four times. In 1965 it was deployed on Operation Power Pack to Santo Domingo in the Dominican Republic to rescue United States nationals trapped during a revolution. In 1968 and 1969 the Division served for 22 months in Vietnam, during which time it was instrumental in crushing the Tet offensive. Two brigade-sized divisional units played a major role in Operation Urgent Fury, the invasion of Grenada in October 1983. Most recently elements of the Division were deployed to Panama as part of Operation Just Cause to bring about the downfall of the corrupt and drug-ridden Noriega regime.

The ability of the 82nd Airborne Division to react with virtually no notice makes it one of the most potent rapid deployment forces in the world.

101st Airborne (Air Assault)

Specialist Insignia: A patch comprising the head of the American bald eagle on a black shield is worn on the left shoulder by all ranks. Parachute qualification wings are worn over the left breast.

History: The 101st Airborne Division (Air Assault) is unique. Formed on 15 August 1942 at Camp Clairborne, Louisiana it saw action in Normandy, at Bastogne, in Holland and near Berchtesgaden before its deactivation in November 1945. By then the "Screaming Eagles," as they were known, had been awarded the Distinguished Unit Citation, the French and Belgian Croix de Guerre and the Dutch Orange Lanyard. Reactivated in 1956, the 1st Brigade was deployed to Vietnam in July 1965 to be followed by the remainder of the division in 1967. As its dependence on helicopter operations grew, the Division was redesignated "Air Mobile", sharing with the 1st Cavalry the dangerous task of offensive support. In October 1974, two years after their withdrawal from Vietnam, the "Screaming Eagles" were formally designated the 101st Airborne Division (Air Assault), a title which they are still proud to hold.

Based today at Fort Campbell, Kentucky they are the standing partners of 82nd Airborne within the XVIII Airborne Corps and as such provide CENTCOM's ready strategic reserve. They were deployed to

Saudi Arabia as part of Operation Desert Shield and later played an important part in Desert Storm. They comprise three parachute infantry brigades, three artillery battalions each with 54 105mm towed howitzers, and a total of 90 TOW-armed AH-1 Cobra attack helicopters.

United States Marine Corps

Badge: A globe, depicting Continental America foremost, with an anchor to the rear, the whole surmounted by an American bald eagle

Specialist Insignia: A Marine Corps emblem surrounded by oak leaves is worn on the buckle of the Dress Blue Belt. Insignia also depicted on buttons and worn on Blues high-collars. A forragere is worn on the left shoulder in units which fought at Belleau Wood in 1918

History: Based on colonial battalions raised by the British in America before the Revolutionary War, the Marine Corps itself was initiated by Act of Congress on 11 July 1798. Under the command of William Ward Burrows, the Corps set up its first headquarters in Philadelphia but in 1800 moved to Washington. In 1806 Marine Barracks, Washington, the present headquarters, was completed.

The Corps remained active throughout the 19th century both at home and abroad. Naval attachments took part in a number of actions against British shipping during the War of 1812. Later land-based detachments were instrumental in securing American victories during the Florida, Indian and Mexican Wars. Formally subordinated to the Navy in 1834, the Corps served in the China Seas during the 1850s and fought, both on land and at sea, throughout the Civil War. In a series of bloody battles at the turn of the century, the Marines liberated Cuba and the Philippines from Spanish rule and provided the United States' contribution to the International Relief Expedition against the Chinese Boxers.

The Marines fought with distinction throughout both World Wars, particularly against the Japanese during the bloody Pacific campaign of 1943 to 1945. They deployed to Korea, when they were awarded independence from, and equal status with, the other armed services, and to Vietnam, where they sustained 12,936 dead and 88,594 wounded in some of the bloodiest operations of the war.

The modern US Marine Corps is approximately 200,000 strong, including 9,700 women.

US Army Aggressor Troops

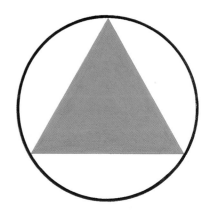

Badge: A white circle with a green equilateral triangle (to denote the fictitious Circle Trigon Party) on either a peaked cap or helmet, reinforced with a ridge running from front to rear

Specialist Insignia: Coloured collar tabs and sleeve patches denoting designated unit (see text)

History: Formed originally in 1946 as a small cadre, Aggressor evolved into a fully fledged mythical enemy with its own uniforms, tactical doctrine, and order of battle.

Signals were even sent in its own language, Esperanto. Defined in Army Regulations as 'a training aid consisting of an imaginary enemy nation with a history, government, armed forces, and an undefined homeland', Aggressor was careful to remain anonymous in the early days. However, as the United States became more heavily embroiled in the Cold War, it inevitably re-configured until at one stage it closely resembled the Soviet Army in its organization, weapons, equipment, uniforms and tactics.

Initially troops attached to Aggressor wore a number of different uniforms to represent their assumed roles and ranks. Paratroopers and Fusilier units, deemed to be élite troops, wore red side hats. Troops assigned to tank and reconnaissance units wore black caps, all others wearing a green helmet with a distinctive ridge running from front to rear over the crest.

Shoulder straps were in three colours – red for fusilier officers, white for marshals and general officers, and green for other officers and all enlisted ranks. Coloured cloth tabs were worn on the collar to designate branch of service, while black Arabic numbers indicated the numerical designation of regimental-sized and smaller units. Divisions were identified by rectangular coloured patches on the upper-right sleeve, with black Arabic numerals to designate the number of the division.

US Army Band (Pershing's Own)

Badge: The band's coat of arms. A shield with crossed sword and baton with a small inset escutcheon commemorating the Rhineland campaign. A five-pointed star within a wreath is above it and a scroll with the words 'Pershing's Own' is below it, the whole in gold

Collar Badges: Crest from the band's coat of arms; worn on the shoulder straps when parading in duty (green) uniform

Badges of Rank: Officers – conventional insignia on shoulder boards in Adjutant-General's Corps colours (dark blue, piped with red); NCOs – gold

History: For the first three years of its history the US Army Band wore olive drab uniforms. However on 6 June 1924 it was issued with blue-gray shade, affectionately known as 'Pershing Gray', in the manner of that worn by officer cadets at the West Point Military Academy. Hot, uncomfortable and unpopular, the uniform was scrapped in 1943 in favour of a slate-blue, summer-weight outfit but was resurrected in 1948 for General Pershing's funeral.

Between 1948 and 1965 when, on its own initiative, it began to develop a completely new uniform, the Band was forced to go from one improvization to another, the victim of apathy and a tightening financial budget. Between 1965 and 1968 a new, more comfortable and far smarter

uniform was introduced, which more completely epitomized the traditions of the US Army as a whole. By way of example, all ranks within the band, except the drum-major, wear a scarlet cap braided with gold to represent the red coats frequently worn by bandsmen up to the time of the Civil War. The drum-major himself parades resplendent in a British Guards officer's-style bearskin with a gold-chain-covered chin strap and white-over-red plume on the left side. His baldric is scarlet, edged with gold and decorated with miniature silver drum-sticks, the band's coat of arms and the 'Rhineland' battle honour in gold.

US Navy SEALS

Specialist Insignia: An eagle with wings spread, clutching a trident, a pistol and an anchor, which is worn on a standard naval uniform in barracks. Operationally Scuba gear appropriate to the environment is issued. A soft floppy hat, rather than the conventional helmet, is worn in combat.

History: The US Navy SEALS were formed on 1 January 1962 after pre-evaluation study had reported the need for an independent group capable of conducting counter-insurgency operations, conventional and clandestine, on land and at sea. Existing Underwater Demolition Teams were then carrying out their duties of reconnaissance, beach and mine clearance excellently but were lacking in their full potential by having no offensive role.

The word SEAL is derived from an acronym for Sea, Air and Land and demonstrates perfectly the sheer depth of ability of the Unit. All members are parachute-trained and are capable of reaching their objective from carrier or land-based aircraft. More usually, however, they are carried close to their target by submarine from which they can make either surface or submerged exits. Once ashore the SEALS can be regarded as a match for any conventional enemy particularly as they invariably have the element of surprise on their side.

There are currently six SEAL teams in commission divided into approximately 70 platoons. SEAL Teams 1, 3 and 5 are

stationed at the Naval Amphibious Base at Coronado, San Diego and 2 and 4 at Little Creek, Norfolk, Virginia. SEAL Team 6, formed in 1980, is specially trained for counter-terrorist operations. Unlike the others, which are under the command of two Naval Special Warfare Groups (known rather unpronounceably as NAVSPECWARGRU 1 and 2), it is controlled directly by the US Navy's Atlantic Command in Norfolk, Virginia.

US 75th Ranger Regiment

Badge: An individual battalion flash superimposed on a six-coloured shield, commemorating the combat teams comprising Merrill's Marauders, on a black beret

Specialist Insignia: A Ranger flash worn on the upper right sleeve is presented to all successful candidates of the Ranger School. The Ranger scroll worn below the flash is awarded only to members of the 75th Ranger Regiment. Parachute qualification wings are worn conventionally above the left breast-pocket

History: The 75th Ranger Regiment draws its traditions from two highly individualistic World War II units. The 75th Infantry Regiment was originally designated the 5307th Composite Unit (Provisional) but soon became universally known as Merrill's Marauders in honour of its dashing and far-sighted commander. Formed in October 1943 specifically for service in Indo-China, the Marauders operated behind Japanese lines throughout the spring and summer of 1944. Reorganized and redesignated the 475th Infantry Regiment in August 1944, the Regiment was deactivated in July 1945, reformed as the 75th Infantry Regiment in June 1954, and deactivated again in March 1966.

The original Rangers, who adopted the name of a team of pre-Independence Indian fighters, were formed in Carrickfergus, Northern Ireland, in 1942. Under the command of Major William Derby, and closely emulating the British Commandos, they took part in the campaigns in North

Africa, Sicily and Italy before returning to England to play a major role in securing the D-Day beaches. Small groups of Rangers fought in the Korean War but were deactivated soon after.

The 75th Infantry Regiment, reformed yet again in January 1969, was designated the 1st Battalion (Ranger) 75th Regiment in 1973 in response to the need for a highly mobile light infantry unit able to operate at minimum notice anywhere in the world. The 2nd Battalion was formed at Fort Lewis, Washington, in October 1974 and the 3rd Battalion at Fort Benning, Georgia, in October 1975. The unit was redesignated the 75th Ranger Regiment in 1975.

US Special Forces

Badge: The Special Forces crest, comprising crossed arrows, a dagger and the motto 'De Oppresso Liber' ('Freedom from Oppression'), worn over the individual group flash on a green beret

Specialist Insignia: Silver wings mounted on a background of teal blue and gold, worn over the left breast to denote parachute qualification. The word 'Airborne' in gold on a green background is worn on the upper shoulders above an arrowhead shoulder patch in green, depicting a vertical knife cut by three lightning flashes

History: The original US-Canadian Special Forces group, raised to operate behind enemy lines during World War II, was disbanded with the coming of peace. During the Cold War years which followed, it became obvious that the West would have difficulty in withstanding the might of the Soviet Union (which had not demobilized) in any future conventional war and that consequently large areas of territory would be overrun. Accordingly it was decided to create a force skilled in guerrilla warfare capable both of harassing the enemy and assisting local resistance groups.

The 10th Special Forces Group (Airborne), commanded by Colonel Aaron Bank, was activated at Fort Bragg, North Carolina, on 20 June 1952 to undertake this role. 77th Special Forces Group was formed in September 1953 and 1st Special Forces Group in 1957. The 5th Special Forces Group, raised in 1961, served throughout most of the conflict in Vietnam, becoming expert in the formation of Civilian Irregular Defence Groups among the semi-nomadic Montagnards.

There are currently eight Special Forces Groups (Airborne) operating worldwide under the control of the 1st Special Operations Command (Airborne). Four of these groups – the 1st, 5th, 7th and 10th – are active, each with a battalion deployed abroad. A further two are in the Reserve and two are in the National Guard.

Army Air Corps

Badge: A silver eagle within a crowned wreath on a square dark blue patch; light blue beret

Pilots: A crowned lion standing on a crown between light blue wings, worn on the left breast

Rank: Senior NCOs wear a light blue eagle, edged in dark blue, above their chevrons. Prior to transferring to the AAC, NCOs on attachment are issued with the light blue beret but continue to wear the cap badge of their parent unit.

History: One of the newer corps of the British Army, the Army Air Corps was formed in September 1957 from the amalgamation of the old Glider Pilot Regiment and the Royal Air Force Observation Post squadrons, the latter then manned by Royal Artillery pilots. Unlike the Royal Navy and Royal Air Force, the AAC uniquely accepts NCO pilots. Selection and training are rigorous. With the exception of a small number of direct-entrant officers, who will be sent to the infantry for six months to gain basic military skills after commissioning, most transferees will have served at least five years in the Army before gaining their wings. Potential NCO pilots must serve at least two years as groundcrewmen and a further two years as aircrewmen, mastering such basics as map reading, air operations, flight servicing and tactics, before even being considered for pilot training.

With the exception of the recently formed 666 Squadron (V) – comprising a combination of retired regular crewmen and civilian pilots and equipped with the old but thoroughly reliable Scout aircraft – operational squadrons fly either the Gazelle or the Lynx helicopter, the latter armed with the United States' TOW wire-guided anti-tank missile.

7th Duke of Edinburgh's Own Gurkha Rifles

Badge: Two crossed silver kukris, points and cutting edge up; between the points '7', between the hilts the reversed crowned cypher 'P'; black pill box hat worn on parade. Rifle-green and black stable belt

Lanyard: Rifle (dark) green and black

History: Until 1947 the ten regiments of Gurkhas were part of the British Indian Army but, with the coming of Indian independence that year, the units were split equally between the new Indian Army, with which some 80,000 still serve, and the British Army. Numbers serving with the British Army have dwindled steadily to a present low of 8,000 officers and men and are due to be halved within the next decade in anticipation of the return of Hong Kong to Chinese rule. The Brigade itself is far larger than any other in the British Army, consisting of a headquarters and three battalions in Hong Kong, a battalion at Church Crookham, near Aldershot in England, and a battalion serving in Brunei at the express wish, and expense, of the Sultan. Uniquely the Brigade had its own engineering, transport and signals support and, until 1971, even had its own independent parachute company. The five infantry battalions (the 1st and 2nd Battalions 2nd King Edward VII's Own Gurkha Rifles, the 6th Queen Elizabeth's Own Gurkha Rifles, the 7th Duke of Edinburgh's Own Gurkha Rifles, and the 10th Princess Mary's Own Gurkha Rifles) take it in turns to serve at Church Crookham, a posting which brings with it a great deal of prestige touched with homesickness for a native land thousands of miles away.

During its tour of duty in England in 1982, the 7th Duke of Edinburgh's Own Gurkha Rifles was assigned to 5th Infantry Brigade and sent to assist in the retaking of the Falklands. Although involved in none of the set-piece battles, the very reputation of the Gurkhas was enough to strike terror in the hearts of the enemy.

The Life Guards

Badge: A gold cypher 'EIIR' within a crowned ring worn on a navy blue beret
Specialist Insignia: Red over blue stable belt, black polo-necked jersey sometimes worn under green coverall
Lanyard: Red, worn on right shoulder
History: The Household Cavalry consists of two regiments, the Life Guards and the Blues and Royals (Royal Horse Guards and the 1st Dragoons). They are the senior regiments of the British Army and fully integrated into its organization.

The Life Guards, who are able to trace their lineage back to the Royalist supporters who followed King Charles II into exile

in Holland in the 17th century, after the English Civil War, are the most senior, if not the oldest, regiment in the British Army. They have mounted bodyguard to the Sovereign for over 300 years and today appear at her side on all ceremonial occasions when she moves in state through the streets of London. More commonly, they can be seen taking turns with their friendly rivals the Blues and Royals in mounting guard at the front and rear of London's aptly-named Horse Guards building.

The regiment is not just a ceremonial unit. It has a distinguished fighting record beginning with its first action at Maastricht

in 1673. Since then it has seen action in all of Britain's major military campaigns. It fought throughout the Napoleonic Wars, culminating in the Battle of Waterloo in 1815, it joined with the Blues to soldier with Wolseley in Egypt in 1882, and earned 28 battle honours in World War I. During World War II, serving as part of the Guards Armoured Division, the Life Guards won a further 21 battle honours. Since 1945 the Regiment has served in Cyprus, in the Middle East in Aden, Palestine and Oman, and in the Far East in Malaya, Singapore and Borneo.

Parachute Regiment

Badge: A silver winged parachute below a crown surmounted by a lion

Specialist Insignia: Maroon beret and stable belt; light blue and white parachutist's badge worn on top of right sleeve

Lanyard: Worn on right shoulder; 1st Battalion red, 2nd Battalion blue, 3rd Battalion green

History: The 'Paras', as Britain's paratroopers are known, were officially formed in September 1941 when the 1st Parachute Brigade, consisting of the 1st, 2nd and 3rd Battalions of the Parachute Regiment, was raised. Specially selected and trained, the force grew until it comprised two complete Airborne Divisions. In the immediate post-war period the Paras were reduced in size, a trend which was destined to continue until the ultimate disbandment of 16 Parachute Brigade in 1974. During the period immediately prior to its dispersal the Brigade was constantly active in overseas campaigns. These included operations in Palestine, Malaya, Cyprus, Suez, the Middle East, Aden and Borneo.

With the disbandment of 16 Parachute Brigade, the three airborne battalions were reduced to filling one 'para-role' slot in rotation. After the Falklands campaign of 1982, in which the 2nd and 3rd Battalions won a brilliant worldwide reputation for aggressive soldiering against great odds, the need for an out-of-area operations brigade was conceded. 5 Airborne Brigade was formed in 1983 and today consists of two of the three parachute battalions plus various para- and airmobile supporting services. The regular Parachute Regiment is enhanced by three Territorial Army battalions.

Royal Artillery

Badge: A brass cannon under a crown and above a scroll bearing the word 'Ubique' (which means 'Everywhere') worn on a navy beret

Specialist Insignia: Red stable belt with dark blue central band having a central yellow stripe; officers and warrant officers

wear dark blue jerseys with 'RA' shoulder titles.

Lanyard: White lanyard on left shoulder

History: The Royal Artillery, or Royal Regiment, was created as an independent force some 400 years ago. As such it is one of the oldest formations in the British Army, and enjoys the privilege of parading on the right of line. The title 'Royal Regiment' is in many ways a misnomer as the Royal Artillery is in reality considerably larger than many corps and actually has its own two-star general, designated Major-General Royal Artillery or MGRA, in over-all command. To add to the confusion, 'The Regiment' is divided into a number of independent fighting units,

themselves referred to as regiments.

The modern artillery is a powerful and complex branch of the Army. It is the only British unit to employ battlefield nuclear weapons, although the Lance missile, deployed by 50 Missile Regiment in support of 1st (British) Corps in West Germany, is soon to disappear as part of the current package of arms reductions.

The traditions of horse-drawn artillery are perpetuated within the ranks of the Royal Horse Artillery, an élite within the Regiment which still retains its own distinctive light blue and yellow striped stable belt and officer's cap badge bearing the royal cypher 'EIIR'.

Royal Military Police

Badge: Brass, depicting the motif 'EIIR' within a crowned laurel wreath; below the wreath a scroll; red beret, lanyard worn on the left, and stable belt. During operations the red beret may be discarded in favour of a conventional navy blue beret

History: The office of Provost Marshal is the oldest in British military history and dates back to the reign of Henry III. The predecessors of the modern Military Police, the Military Mounted Police, were formed in 1887 and were joined five years later by the Military Foot Police. The two separate organizations served with distinction from the Battle of Neuve Chappelle in 1915 until the end of World War I in 1918, sustaining 375 fatalities and winning 477 awards. The two organizations combined in 1926 to become the modern Corps of Military Police.

During World War II the Corps was charged with the maintenance of discipline, the detection of crime, and with traffic control. Its members served in every major theatre, were among the first on the beaches of Normandy, and parachuted into Arnhem.

In 1946 the Corps was granted the prefix 'Royal' and has continued to serve with distinction in every operational theatre involving the British Army. Most recently it has worked closely with the Royal

Ulster Constabulary in Northern Ireland, earning nearly 100 awards and honours for bravery.

Today's Corps is relatively small, a mere 150 officers and 2,250 other ranks including 250 women. It is, however, as potent a force as ever and one wholly capable of living up to its proud motto, 'Exemplo Ducemus' ('We lead by example').

Special Air Service

Badge: A silver dagger with light blue wings and scroll bearing the motif 'Who Dares Wins' on a dark blue patch (raised in the case of an officer) worn on a sand-coloured beret.

Collar badges: Metal winged daggers

Specialist Insignia: SAS straight-topped wings worn on upper right shoulder

Rank: All ranks wear black rank designators above the letters SAS on the shoulder boards

History: The SAS has arguably the finest record in counter-insurgency and low profile operations in the world. Formed by David Stirling in 1941, initially as an adjunct to the Long Range Desert Group, the SAS proved so successful at its behind-the-lines activities that it was expanded steadily throughout the war. By 1945 it comprised five battalions, two British, two French and one Belgian. At the end of the war the Belgian and French regiments were officially handed over to their respective armies, both of which kept them on strength. The British SAS, however, was disbanded. A year later 21 Special Air Services (Artists) Regiment, a Territorial Army unit, was reformed largely from ex-wartime SAS combatants. In 1950, to combat a mounting communist terrorist threat in Malaya, 22 SAS, a regular army battalion, was formed and sent to the Far East. B Squadron was scrapped and the regiment reduced in size after the successful completion of the Malaya campaign in 1960. B Squadron was reformed, and the Regiment augmented by the Guards Independent Parachute Company – later to become G Squadron – when the SAS deployed to Brunei in 1964. Today the Regiment constitutes one regular and two TA battalions.

Special Boat Service

Badge: A standard Royal Marines Commando badge, comprising a globe surrounded by a wreath of laurel leaves surmounted by a crown, is worn on a green beret

Specialist Insignia: The SBS no longer wear the SAS-style straight wings. They now wear standard RM parachute wings above a 'Swimmer-Canoeist' badge, in the form of a crown surmounted by the letters SC flanked by laurel leaves, on the right shoulder

History: Members of the Special Boat Service, until recently the Special Boat Squadron, comprise the Special Forces element of the Royal Marines Commando.

The origins of the SBS lie within the Royal Marines Boom Patrol Detachment, the Combined Operations Beach and Boat Section and the Small Raids Wing which undertook reconnaissance and raiding duties along the European and Far Eastern coastlines throughout World War II. The value of these groups was so self-evident that, unlike the SAS, which was disbanded, the groups survived the post-war cutbacks and amalgamations to form the nucleus of the newly-constituted 'Small Raids Wing' attached to the Royal Marines Amphibious School.

In 1977, in recognition of the consistently high standards achieved by them, they were renamed the Special Boat Squadron. Very recently, in an attempt to streamline the British Army Special Forces capabilities, and in total disregard of their naval traditions and independence, they have been redesignated the Special Boat Service and brought under centralized special forces command.

Belgian Para-Commando Regiment

History: Parachute and commando units were formed in 1942 from the Free Belgian Forces then stationed in the United Kingdom. The first parachute company, drawn from the 2nd Battalion Belgian Fusiliers, was originally incorporated into the British Parachute Regiment but was subsequently redesignated the Belgian Independent Parachute Company in January 1943. A year later it became the Belgian Squadron of the Special Air Service Brigade. After the Liberation it was increased to battalion status and in April 1945 formally designated 5SAS. It was posted to Germany as part of the army of occupation in April 1946, assuming the title 1er Régiment Parachutiste-SAS.

The Belgian Commandos were formed on 30 April 1942 as 4 Troop of 10 (Inter-Allied) Commando attached initially to 2 Commando Brigade. After the war the unit, now based at March-les-Dames, was renamed the Belgian-Commando Unit.

A founder member of NATO, Belgium was quick to send the Corps Voluntaires Corea (CVC), drawn from volunteers from the Commando and Parachute Regiments, to support the United Nations in Korea. While there, the CVC not only saw considerable action but paved the way for ultimate amalgamation.

In February 1952, unification was agreed in principle; in April the regiments were redesignated battalions, and in May the Parachute-Commando Regiment was formed. Great care was taken to ensure that neither unit was forced to compromise its traditions, and each retained its coveted maroon or green beret.

Badge: 1 Parachute Battalion – SAS winged dagger on cap and maroon beret; 2 and 4 Commando Battalions – dagger cap badge and dagger and scroll on green beret; 3 Parachute Battalion – coat-of-arms badge on cap and on maroon beret

Specialist Insignia: 1 and 3 Parachute Battalions – maroon collar patch with light blue piping; 2 and 4 Commando Battalions – black collar patch with white piping. Officers and senior NCOs wear shoulder slides with collar patch colours, pipings and rank insignia

1/22 Airborne Regiment (Czechoslovakia)

Badge: A lion cap badge worn on a red beret on parade, or dark grey-brown beret in the field

Specialist Insignia: Regimental patch depicting golden parachute with sky-blue-and-white lower background within a white-edged red oval, the whole within a yellow diamond, worn on the left sleeve. With working dress, badges of rank are worn above the right breast pocket; with parade dress they are worn with silver arm-of-service insignia on the shoulder boards

History: Czechoslovakia has an airborne tradition dating back to World War II when Free Czechs fought with the 'London' and 'Moscow Armies' against Nazi Germany. Czech agents were dropped into their homeland throughout 1941 and 1942 to keep alive the spirit of resistance, culminating on 27 May 1942 in the assassination of Reinhard Heydrich, Hitler's deputy and one of the most powerful men in the Third Reich.

The Red Army liberated most of Czechoslovakia in 1945, remaining in occupation until the end of the year. A fledgling Czechoslovak People's Army ('Ceskoslovenska Lidova Armada') was set up but was powerless to prevent a Communist Party takeover in 1948.

Prior to 1968 the army was considered one of the better trained and equipped within the non-Soviet Warsaw Pact. The 'Prague Spring' and the subsequent Soviet-inspired invasion by Czechoslavakia's hard-line communist neighbours, proved to be the undoing of the Army, which was never wholly trusted again. Five Soviet divisions were sent to Czechoslovakia on a temporary basis to ensure the maintenance of 'normality' and are only now being withdrawn.

Although it was given little in the way of equipment, the Czech Airborne Brigade was allowed to continue. Today the 7th Airborne Battalion, based at Holleschau, and the 1st Battalion, 22nd Airborne regiment, are regarded as élite, the latter given special forces status.

Légionnaire, 2e Rep, France

Badge: Gold grenade worn on beret or ceremonially on kepi (white for ordinary soldiers, black for officers and NCOs)

Specialist Insignia: Parachute insignia of stylized wings with central parachute, worn on the right breast. A blue cummerbund, worn beneath a standard-issue webbing belt, denotes 2e REP

History: One of the most legendary and romantic formations in the world, the Légion Etrangère, or Foreign Legion, came into being on 9 March 1831. Initially composed entirely of foreign nationals officered by French citizens, the Legion soon proved itself to be one of the most capable and versatile fighting forces of the world.

The modern Legion comprises a highly trained, fully integrated armed force capable of operating anywhere and boasting its own infantry, armour, engineers and support units. No element is more dedicated or professional than the Legion's own Parachute Regiment – 2e Régiment Etranger de Parachutistes.

The Regiment's history dates back to the French involvement in Indo-China (now Vietnam) during the 1950s when the unit, then designated 2e Bataillon Etranger de Parachutistes, was virtually wiped out during the siege of Dien Bien Phu.

After being reformed, the Regiment saw extensive service in Algeria before being recalled to the French island of Corsica in 1963. Shortly thereafter 2e REP, as it was now designated, relinquished the role of conventional airborne infantry in favour of that of Para-Commando. Today it forms an integral part of 11e Division Parachutiste, itself a key part of the Force de l'Action Rapide.

With entry no longer barred to the French, 2e REP is now a truly international organization with up to 50 nationalities represented. A large percentage of its membership is, however, English speaking, mostly British but with a number from the United States, Canada, South Africa and Australia.

Parachute Regiment, France

Badge: A circled wing, sword and star worn on a blue beret

Specialist Insignia: Metal or embroidered wire wings (Basic, Moniteur and HALO) are worn together with badges of rank over the right breast pocket (metal wings have a small plaque on the reverse where the holder's award number may be stamped)

History: France has one of the largest and most experienced airborne forces in the world. Indeed during the last 30 years 'les paras', as they have come to be known, have earned themselves a reputation for tenacity and toughness second to none. Prior to World War II, France's paratroopers were a part of the French Air Force. L'Armée de l'Air and the Army's first airborne units were not formed until 1956, since when they have seen action in Egypt, Indo-China, Algeria and Central Africa.

France's present airborne division, the 11e Division Parachutiste was formed in 1971 from 11e Division d'Intervention and the 20e and 25e Parachute Brigades and now comprises 13,000 men. It is a completely integrated airborne division with its own command, transport and supply facilities and constitutes the largest element within the Force de l'Action Rapide (FAR). Comprising five divisions, 47,000 troops and equipped as it is with the latest weapons and communications, all or part of the Force de l'Action Rapide, commensurate with the scale of the threat, can go anywhere in the world and is capable of fighting under most conditions.

Greek Parachute Regiment

Badge: A white Hellenic Cross on a blue shield background surrounded by a gold wreath, worn on a green beret

Specialist Insignia: Officers and NCOs wear collar patches depicting crossed rifles with a wreath in gold on a red background. Parachute Regiment insignia and tabs worn on either shoulder. If awarded, Free Faller badges are worn above the left breast pocket

History: Greek parachute troops can trace their origins back to 1942 and the formation of the Greek Sacred Squadron. Composed of ex-commissioned volunteers who agreed to serve in the ranks, the raiding unit was incorporated into the British SAS in North Africa and participated in several major raids against the Afrika Corps. In March 1942 the highly effective force was attached to the New Zealand Corps, equipped with some 30 heavily armed jeeps, and tasked with executing a complex flanking move against the Tunisian Mareth Line. With the war in North Africa over, the Greeks were attached to the British Special Boat Squadron with whom they undertook several brilliantly executed raids against the occupied islands.

The Sacred Squadron was disbanded with the coming of peace, but a new parachute school was opened in 1955.

Above: Printed parachute wings are worn above the left breast pocket. The star within a wreath indicates the grade of master instructor.

Sponsored and equipped by the United States, Greek instructors received training at Fort Benning, Georgia. Officers and senior NCOs received Ranger as well as parachute qualifications.

Currently, Greece has a Parachute Regiment of three battalions incorporated into the Parachute-Commando Division. One battalion is designated a Special Raider Force in recognition of the debt owed to the original Greek Sacred Squadron.

The Folgore Brigade (Italy)

Badge: An Airborne badge representing a parachute within a set of wings is worn by all members of the brigade whether or not they are qualified paratroopers. Berets are maroon for paratroopers (including a Carabinieri battalion), cornflower blue for army aviation, green for Laguneri and black for all others

Specialist Insignia: Brigade patch worn above the badge of rank on a brassard on the left shoulder. Parachutists' badges are worn on the right breast. Silver 'Savoy' stars with winged parachute and dagger may be worn on the collar. The background colour indicates function within the brigade; black with gold edging for artillery, black with red edging for engineers, maroon for medics, medium blue for non-specialists

History: Italy was among the pioneers of military parachuting and formed a fully equipped parachute company as early as 1938. Two battalions, each of 250 men, fought in the unsuccessful Libya campaign and were joined in 1940 by a third battalion. Plans were formulated for an airborne assault on Malta but never put into effect. All three battalions joined with their logistics support in 1942 to form the Folgore Brigade but were never exploited to their full potential. Indeed it was not until after their surrender in 1943, when part of the Brigade reformed as 'F' Squadron, part of the British 8th Army, that they saw strenuous service.

After the war the Italians retained a nucleus of airborne troops, reforming the Parachute School at Tarquinia in 1946. A Parachute Brigade, later designated the Folgore Brigade, was formed in 1952. Uniquely, Folgore has its own Airborne Carabinieri battalion together with an Alpini Parachute Company. The 9th 'Colonel Moschin' Assault (Saboteur) Parachute Battalion, the special forces of the Italian Army, form part of the Brigade.

Royal Netherlands Marine Corps

Badge: A gold anchor badge with a red background worn on a black beret. (Army Commandos wear green berets with a crossed Fairbairn-Sykes dagger badge)

Specialist Insignia: Qualification badges; red SCUBA tank and fins on a black background or gold dolphins on a black background for combat swimmers, red star on a black background for snipers, British-style 'wings' for paratroopers, white stag on a black-and-white shield for winter warfare specialists

History: The Royal Netherlands Marine Corps (RNLMC) is the oldest unit within the Netherlands Armed Forces, with a proud tradition dating back to 1665 when it was formed to fight the English. Traditionally the RNLMC supported Holland's huge mercantile fleet, particularly in the East Indies and China Sea. More recently, Dutch Marines were instrumental in delaying the initial German advance across the Maas River in 1940.

Many Marines managed to escape to Britain after the fall of Holland and at once enlisted into the Free Dutch Forces. The Princess Irene Brigade, which took an active part in the D-Day landings and in the subsequent drive through North-west Europe, contained a strong Marine element. After the War the Corps was expanded and saw further action in the protracted East Java campaign.

The modern Corps has its headquarters in Rotterdam, although the crack anti-terrorist unit, responsible for a series of actions against the South Moluccan terrorists, is stationed at the Van Braam Houckgeest Barracks in Doorn. Today, the all-volunteer, and almost exclusively regular, RNLMC has a strength of 2,800, including 170 officers and 800 NCOs.

Polish Air Assault Division

Badge: A silver braid Piast eagle worn centrally on a red beret (based on the Polish Imperial Eagle without the crown). Rank insignia worn to left of cap badge

Specialist Insignia: Parachute insignia worn over right breast-pocket (open parachute on green background surmounted by an eagle for basic paratroopers; larger, fully deployed parachute with a diving eagle holding a gold wreath for instructors). Divisional patch, denoting a deployed parachute with a soaring eagle and wreath, all in white against a red circular background, worn on the left upper arm. (A large number of battalion and even company variations of the basic colour have been noted)

History: The 6th Pomeranian Airborne Division was created in 1957 and now forms the largest non-Soviet airborne unit in Eastern Europe. Although the Polish People's Army ('Ludowe Wojsko Polskie') was itself formed only in 1941, and was not fully modernized until 1946, its airborne traditions are among the oldest in the world. The Bydgoszez Military Parachute School was formed as long ago as 1938; small groups attached to the Red Army dropped behind enemy lines to aid the Communist-inspired Polish resistance from 1943 and the 1st Polish Independent Parachute Brigade courageously jumped to virtual annihilation in support of the British Airborne Forces at Arnhem in 1944.

The red beret was selected for the 6th PDPD (Pomorska Dywizja Powietrzna-Desantowa) in 1963 on the astonishing misapprehension that the wartime Independent Parachute Brigade, which had always proudly worn its traditional pale blue-grey colours, had for some reason worn British airborne maroon berets at Arnhem.

7th Polish Naval Assault Division

Badge: A large silver Imperial eagle, minus the crown, is worn on a blue beret. Rank insignia is worn to the left of the badge

Specialist Insignia: A divisional patch depicting a white anchor and wreath within a blue white-edged circle is worn on the upper arm

History: Despite its rather misleading title, the 7th Naval Assault Division ('Luzcyka Dywizyz Desantnowa-Morska' – 7LDDM) is not under naval jurisdiction but is in fact a part of the Polish Army. Formed in 1967 from the amalgamation of the 23rd Mechanized Division and the 3rd Marine Regiment. 7LDDM is now based in the thriving sea port of Gdansk, where it comes under the nominal jurisdiction of the

Pomeranian Military District based in Bydgoszez. The role of the Division has been called into some doubt recently by the massive change in Poland's political outlook. Although referred to internally by the euphemism 'Jadnostka Obrona Wybrzeza', or coastal defence unit, the role of the unit is almost exclusively offensive. Trained to assist Soviet and East German troops in the rapid neutralization of Denmark and southern Norway in a war against NATO, the Division is now finding itself without a natural enemy and, by implication, without a *raison d'être*. Although traditionally believed to be politically reliable by the Communist establishment (7LDDM has always been regarded as apolitical despite the proximity of its headquarters to the volatile Gdansk shipyards), the future role of this militarily excellent unit must be regarded at the best as tenuous.

Fallschirmjäger (West Germany)

Badge: A diving eagle within a wreath on a red beret

Specialist Insignia: High jump boots and a modified helmet are issued. The Airborne insignia comprises a silver parachute within a wreath and a set of wings. The colour of the wreath varies according to qualification. Shoulder tabs are red. A white parachute within a blue shield is worn on the left upper arm by paratroopers attached to the Airborne Division

History: Germany was one of the first countries to recognize the usefulness of airborne troops and established a Parachute School at Stendal airbase as early as January 1936. By the outbreak of war, Germany possessed a full airborne brigade and had already actively deployed 50 paratroopers to Spain to fight alongside Franco in the Condor Legion. In the early stages of the war the Fallschirmjäger, as the paratroopers were known, played an important part in the initial German offensives, including the invasions of Czechoslavakia, Denmark, Norway and the Low Countries. It was not until the invasion of Crete in 1941 that the use of German airborne forces was restricted. Although the massive airborne invasion was successful, the casualties sustained were so high (over 4,000 men) that the Fallschirmjäger were rarely deployed again. The Ramcke Parachute Brigade, designated for the invasion of Malta, was committed to ground fighting in North Africa, while the 1st Parachute Division was relegated to a High Command reserve in France.

When the West German Army, the Bundeswehr, was reformed in 1955, it was decided to create an Airborne Brigade. Trained initially by the United States, the West Germans were quick to learn and were soon competent enough to open their own school at Altenstadt/Schongau. The brigade was expanded to a division and its headquarters moved to Esslingen in January 1957.

Panzergrenadier (West Germany)

Badge: A silver Marder APC above crossed rifles within a wreath, worn on a dark green beret

Specialist Insignia: National flag worn on the left shoulder. Bright green shoulder and lapel badges. Light grey woven rank insignia worn on shoulder slides

History: Germany was the first country to develop the modern mechanised infantryman. In 1939 the German Army, 'Das Heer', had a total of 39 infantry divisions including four mechanized divisions designated the 2nd, 13th, 20th and 29th. These divisions were among the vanguard of the German fighting machine and an important part of the *blitzkrieg* offensive policy. Initially the ten Panzer Divisions, the hitting power of the German Army, consisted of two complete tank regiments, totalling some 400 tanks, a small infantry complement and service support elements. During the successful invasion of France in June 1940, the Panzer units far outran the infantry to such an extent that the latter units were unable to keep in contact with, or support, the tanks. The situation was soon redressed, so that by the end of that year each Panzer Division had been reorganised to incorporate one tank regiment, two motorized infantry regiments, two motorized infantry regiments and stronger, more mobile artillery.

In addition to the motorized infantry

attached to the Panzer Divisions, the order of battle included specialized Panzer Grenadier Brigades comprising two mechanized infantry regiments, usually of two companies each. Soon after the fall of France, one company per regiment was equipped with armoured half-tracked vehicles to enhance mobility. These companies were the forerunners of the modern Panzer Grenadiers.

Airborne Regiment USSR

Badge: A red star containing a small hammer and sickle within a gold wreath, worn on a blue beret (the beret is replaced when jumping or when operating in extreme temperatures)

Specialist Insignia: Badges of rank worn above the letters CA on blue shoulder boards. Blue collar tabs with gold insignia parachutes. Blue and white striped (élite forces) shirts. A blue shield depicting a deployed parachute, two aircraft and red star with gold edging containing an embossed hammer and sickle, the whole within a gold surround, is worn on the upper sleeves. Guards insignia is worn over the right breast

History: The Soviet Union was one of the first major countries to recognize the potential of highly trained airborne troops. Between August 1930, when a platoon executed the first successful parachute attack against a corps headquarters, and the outbreak of The Great Patriotic War (1941-45), the 'Vozdushov Desantiye Voyska', or Soviet Airborne Forces, grew steadily. By 1941 the Soviets were able to field 12 first-line airborne brigades and in 1942 actually dropped an entire division of 10,000 men behind enemy lines.

Since the war the VDV has continued growing until today there are some 50,000 men deployed with eight divisions, six combat-ready, one reserve and one cadre. All are stationed on the Soviet borders, four in the Baltic and north-west, two in the west, one in the south-west and one,

the 6th Guards Air Assault Division, in the south-east.

The VDV has long been used by the Government as its iron fist whenever circumstances dictated. The 103rd Guards Air Assault Division spearheaded the invasion of Czechoslovakia in 1968 and supported the 105th Guards Air Assault Division in the capture of Kabul in December 1979.

Most recently the VDV has been used in an internal security role in an attempt to contain ethnic unrest in the volatile Soviet south-west. It proved less than fit for the role and has perhaps placed a question mark against its future. In the growing climate of international reconciliation it is highly likely that one, if not 'more, of its divisions will soon be scrapped.

KGB

Badge: A hammer and sickle within a gold-edged red star supported by a wreath, worn on a variety of hats including the fur shapka for ceremonial occasions. Peaked caps are green-topped for Border Guards and blue-topped for the Internal Army

Specialist Insignia: Collar tabs and shoulder boards are green for border guards and blue for interior forces. Shoulder boards for sergeants and below are inscribed with PV for Border Guards. The KGB Ceremonial Guard parades in officer-issue uniforms

History: The Komitet Gosudarstvennoi Bezopastnosti, the Committee of State Security, came into being on 13 March 1954 to replace the notorious and feared NKVD. Under Andropov's leadership in the 1970s, it began to dismantle much of the secrecy which had surrounded it and even published books for domestic consumption. Since then it has steadily become more open, even allowing television cameras into its headquarters.

The exact size of the KGB is unknown, but it is thought to consist of approxi-

mately 230,000 officers and men, of whom a staggering 170,000 are conscripts serving for three years in lieu of conventional military service.

The largest KGB formation is the Border Guard, comprising some 150,000 soldiers. Responsible for the protection of the Soviet Union's external and internal borders, and not the East/West border as is often assumed, it is recruited on the basis of competitive examination but has a marked Russian, Byelorussián and Ukranian bias. The Internal Army is less overt, although it does contain within its ranks the much-photographed Ceremonial Guard responsible for mounting guard over Lenin's tomb.

MVD

Badge: A golden hammer and sickle within a gold-edged red star superimposed on silver laurel leaves, usually worn on a black peaked cap with russet band
Specialist Insignia: Rank worn on russet shoulder boards. Sergeants and below have the letters BB
History: In the best traditions of the Soviet Union, the MVD, responsible for the maintenance of internal order, operates completely independently of the Armed Forces. Reputedly some 260,000 strong, the Interior Army, or Vnutrennie Voiska, maintains its own armour, APCs, and artillery. Traditionally, the bulk of the MVD has always been drawn from politically reliable members of the less privileged minorities in the belief that it would offer little sympathy to troublemakers in the more affluent western Soviet republics. In practice, it proved virtually impotent when called upon to crush the sectarian rioting in the south-west during the latter stages of 1989.

A secondary and more sinister role of the MVD is to guard the Gulags, the highly secretive system of labour camps still in existence deep within the Soviet wastelands. Although the worst camps have now been closed and political dissension no longer merits imprisonment, the Soviet penal code is harsh and uncompromising and it is likely that it will be many years before the entire Gulag system is scrapped.

In addition, MVD troops are tasked with guarding vulnerable targets such as industrial plants, bridges, railway stations and airports. Although this may seem paranoid, the Soviets have never lost their fundamental xenophobia, and although in part the guards are positioned to stop the very real threat of pilfering, they are far more concerned with sabotage.

Soviet Motor Rifle Regiment

Badge: A hammer and sickle within a red star supported by a wreath, worn on service dress hat, fur chapka or summer hat, dependent upon climate and conditions

Specialist Insignia: NCO badges of rank worn on red-coloured shoulder boards above the letters CA (sergeants and below only). Coloured collar tabs denote regimental (not battalion) branch of service to which the soldier's unit is subordinated: red – mechanized infantry; black – artillery, tanks, rocket forces; light blue – airborne; green – KGB border troops; blue – KBG internal troops; russet – MVD

History: The 'Workers and Peasants' Red Army', the direct forebear of the modern Soviet Armed Forces, was created on 15 January 1918 from a caucus of ideologically motivated workers. Intended to be the nucleus of a nation in arms, the infant Red Army found itself initially no match for the disciplined White counter-revolutionaries. The need for a large army trained along conventional lines was begrudgingly conceded and conscription introduced. By 1920 the regular forces were some 5,500,000 strong. With the coming of peace, the Red Army was reduced to a professional cadre supported by a conscript territorial militia of some 560,000. During the 1930s Stalin steadily rebuilt the Red Army along traditional lines until, by 1937, it boasted 1,300,000 regulars and 1,500,000 active reservists. Despite its size, the Stalinist purges ensured that the Red Army remained backward-looking. In December 1939, during one month of the Finnish Winter War, it sustained 200,000 casualties. During the Great Patriotic War (1941-45) the Soviet people lost an estimated 23 million dead, one fifth of the entire population.

Peace brought with it an uncompromising desire on the part of all Soviets to ensure that such a catastrophe should never happen again. The Red Army did not demobilize but remained strong and moved vast forces into the satellite states to its west. For the next forty years the Soviets perpetuated a state of Cold War against the

Above: Traditionally this distinctive arm badge was worn on the right upper arm of all uniforms. However, it is now only worn on dress uniforms.

West, maintaining vast tank-heavy armies ready to strike against NATO. With the coming of Gorbachev and *perestroika*, much has changed. The modern Soviet Army is far more defensive in character. Large numbers of tanks have been pulled back in reserve and the motor rifleman has once again returned to predominance.

Soviet Naval Infantry

A badge depicting a gold anchor within a red-edged circle is worn on the left sleeve

History: Although the smallest of the Soviet Union's élite forces, the Naval Infantry is the oldest, tracing its history back to the maritime might of Peter the Great. During the Great Patriotic War (1941-45) it expanded to 350,000 personnel, in 40 brigades and six independent regiments, but saw little action because of the relative inactivity of the Soviet Fleet. Although five naval brigades were awarded Guards status, only four divisional-strength land-ings were made, the majority of the 114 recorded amphibious assaults being of company strength or less.

Disbanded in 1947, the Naval Infantry was reformed in 1961 to guard the huge new naval bases then being built and to operate as dedicated infantry for Admiral Gorshkov's growing 'blue-water' fleet. Today the Naval Infantry consists of a small division and three regiments attached one each to the major fleets, together with an active and highly secretive Naval Spetsnaz element.

Badge: A red star on a black background within a white circle for other ranks, a gold orb supported by a wreath surmounted by a red star for officers. Usually worn on a black beret; when a helmet is worn, it has a five-pointed red star lightly stencilled on the front

Specialist Insignia: Red triangle with gold anchor (denoting Red Banner fleet status) worn on either side of the beret or helmet. Guards insignia badge worn over right breast-pocket. Badges of rank in gold on black shoulder boards. Blue and white striped (élite forces) shirt worn by all ranks.

Australian Special Air Service Regiment

Badge: A silver dagger with light blue wings above a scroll inscribed 'Who Dares Wins'

Collar Badges: Metal winged daggers

Specialist Insignia: SAS straight-topped wings worn on upper right shoulder

Rank: All ranks wear black rank designators above the letters SASR on the shoulder boards

History: The 1st Australian Special Air Services Company was raised at Campbell Barracks, Swarbourne, near Perth, in July 1957. It was almost immediately assimilated into the Royal Australian Regiment, the principal regular infantry regiment of the Army, but regained its independence on 4 September 1964, when it was expanded and reconstituted as the Australian Special Air Services Regiment. Growth continued steadily, until by 1966 the Regiment could boast three 'Sabre' squadrons, a headquarters, base squadron and elements of 151 Signals Squadron.

In 1965, 1 SAS Squadron deployed to Brunei in support of a larger British force then countering Indonesian infiltration, being replaced a year later by 2 Squadron operating in the Kuching area on the Sarawak coast.

Simultaneously the Regiment was committed to Vietnam, one 'Sabre' Squadron at a time serving in the Phuoc Tuy province south-east of Saigon. Between 1966 and the Australian withdrawal in 1971, the Squadrons not only worked in unison with the New Zealanders, providing long-range intelligence and springing ambushes deep behind enemy lines, but operated as a 'fire brigade' reserve offering the conventional infantry fire-support and expertise. Far less secretive than its British equivalent, the Australian SASR does not shun publicity.

Royal 22e Régiment

Badge: A brass beaver with central coat of arms surrounded by the words 'Régiment Canadien-Français' within a red circle. Above the circle is a crown, and below are the words 'Je Me Souviens' ('I Remember')

Collar Badges: A silver fleur-de-lis above a triple scroll inscribed 'Régiment Canadien-Français' (silver for officers, white metal for other ranks)

Shoulder Badge: Brass depicting 'R 22e R' for WO2s and below, silver depicting 'R 22 R' surmounted by a crown for officers and WO1s

History: 22nd (French-Canadian) Battalion was formed on 7 November 1914 for service with the Canadian Expeditionary Force on the Western Front. It fought as part of the 5th Infantry Brigade, 2nd Canadian Division, throughout most of the major campaigns of World War I, winning for itself a number of awards for gallantry including two Victoria Crosses.

The Regiment was disbanded on 20 May 1919 but, because of its outstanding war service, was reformed as an entirely French-Canadian entity on 1 April 1920. Designated the 22nd Regiment, it was redesignated The Royal 22nd Regiment on 1 June 1921 and renamed the Royal 22e Régiment on 15 June 1928.

During World War II the 'Van Doos', as the Regiment came to be known, fought in Sicily, Italy and North-West Europe. In 1950 it formed part of the Canadian UN contingent in Korea and has since undertaken a number of UN peace-keeping duties. While the regimental uniform is markedly British, the mascot is a goat and the dress uniform is similar to that of the old Royal Welch Fusiliers to which it was affiliated, the traditions, including the language used at all times, are wholly French.

Chinese People's Liberation Army

Badge: A red star with silver edging containing Chinese lettering in silver, on a blue circular background with silver edging. Usually worn on Western-style headdress, although old-style 'liberation hats' are retained by some units as working uniform

Specialist Insignia: Red collar tabs with silver-edged red stars. Certain units wear hat bands coloured according to the branch of service. Officers' badges of rank, worn conventionally on the shoulder, have now been reintroduced

History: The Chinese People's Liberation Army is presently undergoing tremendous changes in both personnel and equipment. The one-time reliance on sheer numbers, epitomized by the Korean War, has now been replaced by a yearning for modern technology, much of it Western. The exact size and organization of the PLA remains largely a matter of conjecture. However, the latest figures available would suggest that it is approximately 2,300,000 strong, supported by a People's Militia of 4,300,000 and by the People's Armed Police, numbering some 5,000,000. The strategic nuclear forces, otherwise known as the Second Artillery or Strategic Rocket Forces, account for a further 90,000 personnel. Recent reductions, although admittedly large, are partly cosmetic. By way of example, 300,000 railway construction

troops have recently been taken out of the military ambit and transferred to the civil authorities.

The recent demobilization of a large number of senior officers has proved unpopular with those affected. It has, however, created vacancies for the younger career officers whose prestige is steadily increasing. The habit of voting officers

into power has ceased, and all now wear badges of rank.

The PLA emerged from the Tianenmen Square massacre relatively unscathed, the basis of its power and its relationship with the Communist Party remaining uncompromised. It is likely to play an increasing role in Chinese political decision-making in the years to come.

Chinese People's Navy

Badge: A gold-edged red star with Chinese numerics over an anchor, the whole within a gold-edged black circle

Specialist Insignia: Gold anchor on black shoulder board worn by enlisted ranks; red star over gold anchor on blue shoulder board worn by officers. Blue striped vests worn by enlisted ranks; dark blue lapel boards with gold star and edging worn by officers

History: The Chinese People's Navy, including the Coast Defence, Naval Air and Marine elements, is estimated to be approximately 360,000 officers and sailors strong, of whom some 115,000 are conscripts. It deploys three main fleets (the North, East and South Sea Fleets) and operates 25 coastal defence districts. Still relatively unsophisticated, it has yet to establish a true blue-water presence. Most of its 115 submarines, 19 destroyers and 34 frigates are old, although a new class of fast destroyer is currently building and the fleet does possess three nuclear-powered and one nuclear-armed submarine.

Politically the Navy is poorly served in the corridors of power, with only four dedicated representatives, one in the Politburo and three in the Party's Central Committee. Strangely, the Navy is not represented on the Council of the Ministry of National Defence.

In line with the Chinese defence forces as a whole, the Navy is presently undergoing considerable restructuring. A radical reorganization of the Marines has already taken place, with the force reduced from some nine regiments and 56,000 men to just one brigade of some 4,500.

Airborne Brigade: Israeli Defence Forces

Badge: A standard infantry badge worn on a red beret (or hat for women). Members of certain Sayeret (Reconnaissance) units wear black berets

Specialist Insignia: Parachute wings ('Knafei Tznicha') are worn above the left breast pocket. Those entitled wear the recon wings ('Knafei Sayeret') immediately below. Background colours vary; green for recon, white for instructors, blue for paratroopers and red for those who have jumped operationally. The operational service pin ('Sayeret Shaked') is worn over the right breast-pocket

History: The Israeli paratroops were formed on 26 May 1948 during the War of Independence. Initially the force consisted of a loose collection of British-trained soldiers, resistance fighters, holocaust survivors and the occasional mercenary. During its first few years the unit grew steadily in size and reputation until, by 1955, it had expanded into the 202nd Brigade.

After more years of reprisal raids into Arab territory, the paratroopers were involved in the Six Days War of 1967 in which they spearheaded the capture of Gaza and the Suez Canal and were instrumental in the recapturing of the Old City of Jerusalem.

After that war, a succession of increasingly daring raids were undertaken, including that against the PLO headquarters in Jordan in 1968, the capture of a complete Soviet radar installation in 1969, and the rescue of highjacked hostages in Lod Airport in 1972. During the Yom Kippur War of 1974, they were involved in desperate fighting to stem the Egyptian attack before going on the offensive, and in 1976 gained world-wide respect when they successfully rescued all but one hostage from the grips of Arab terrorists at Entebbe.

Today the Israeli Defence Forces maintain three regular paratroop brigades, the 202nd, 890th and 50th Na'ha'l, as well as three reserve brigades.

Above: Specialist pins are worn above the left breast pocket. If awarded, parachute wings will be worn above the pin.

Golani Infantry Brigade (Israel)

Badge: A conventional bronze infantry badge depicting a dagger entwined by a wreath above a scroll, worn on a brown beret. (Brown head-dress is also issued to women attached to the brigade.) Most troops wear the 'Kova Raful' field-hat when operational

Specialist Insignia: The Golani tunic pin (a tree superimposed on a horizontal knife) is worn on the left breast-pocket flap. Troops who have served in the Lebanon wear a red background to the pin and the Lebanon campaign medal immediately below. High quality, exceptionally light ELBA boots are issued exclusively to the Golani Brigade

History: Of the 12 infantry brigades comprising the bulk of the Israeli Defence Forces, only the Golani Brigade has regular army status. Unlike the reserve brigades, which train in close cooperation with the armoured and artillery wings, Golani has maintained its independence. As such it is ideally suited to execute crucial, if small-scale, quick reaction duties and consequently, since its inception, has almost certainly seen more action than any other unit within the IDF.

Most soldiers within the brigade have served at least one tour in the Lebanon. A few of the older, more experienced veterans may even have taken part in the raid on Entebbe when elements of the brigade were landed to neutralize the airport perimeter guards.

Despite its regular army status, the Golani Brigade contains a high percentage of conscripts undertaking their period of national service. In its infancy the Brigade suffered markedly from the social, economic and political divergence of its conscripts, many of whom were recent immigrants from countries as far afield as the United States, the Soviet Union and Germany. More recently, however, a series of hard-fought battles and anti-terrorist actions have successfully installed into the Unit a sense of purpose and *élan* second to none in the Middle East.

New Zealand Special Air Services

Badge: A vertical dagger, hilt uppermost, with a pair of wings below the hilt. Below, a scroll inscribed 'Who Dares Wins'

Collar Badges: Smaller version of cap badge in silver and gilt

History: The New Zealand Special Air Service Squadron was originally formed in 1955 under the command of Major Frank Rennie. From its inception, the Squadron was closely associated with both the British 22nd and Australian Special Air Service Regiments and to this day wears black web belts and anklets whenever webbing is worn, in order to emphasize the link.

During the 1950s, 22 SAS was deployed in Malaya fighting Communist guerrillas. C Squadron, Rhodesian SAS, initially fought alongside the British but was subsequently withdrawn and replaced by the newly-formed New Zealand unit. The New Zealanders operated very effectively in Malaya, spending eighteen months of their two years operational deployment in the jungle. Strong discipline and very effective training meant that during the unit's tour it sustained only one fatal casualty, while destroying numerous terrorist bases and gaining invaluable intelligence.

Despite earning a high reputation, the unit was disbanded upon its return to New Zealand. It was reformed in 1959, becoming a separate corps. In 1962 a small Squadron was sent to Thailand, operating alongside US Special Forces. To celebrate its famous American forebears, the Forest Rangers, the unit was renamed the 1st Ranger Squadron, New Zealand Special Air Service, on 1 September 1963. No 4 Troop was deployed to South Vietnam in December 1968 and, after initial training in Malaysia, undertook regular reconnaissance and ambush patrols as a troop of the Australian SAS Squadron until withdrawn in February 1971. The Corps reverted to its original title of 1 NZSAS Squadron on 1 April 1978.

Above: In the tradition of the SAS, straight topped wings are worn on the upper right shoulder by all operational troops. They are retained by the wearer even after he returns to his original unit.

Sultan's Special Forces (Oman)

Badge: Straight-topped wings superimposed by crossed scimitars and a circular shield, the whole above a scroll and below a crown. The badge is gold coloured and worn on a lavender beret

Specialist Insignia: Stylized wings are worn on the upper right shoulder. A white parachute is surmounted by a maroon and gold crown, the whole superimposed over crossed scimitars and a set of straight topped blue and grey wings, on a dark blue background

History: Prior to 1970, when Sultan Qaboos bin Said, a Sandhurst-trained Anglophile, seized power from his father in a bloodless coup, Oman was an economic and social backwater. Slavery, albeit on a small scale, was still practised, higher education (particularly for women) was discouraged, and all foreigners, with the exception of a few British advisers, were banned. In the south, the Dhofaris were waging a protracted and successful civil war.

Sultan Qaboos immediately set about enlarging and restructuring his armed forces along British lines. Heavily assisted by the British SAS, and with financial and military support from Iran and Saudi Arabia, the Omanis destroyed the final vestiges of the communist-inspired and Yemeni-backed rebellion in 1975.

In 1977, as part of a major restructuring policy, the Sultan's Armed Forces were split into separate army, navy and air force commands. In 1981 a Chief of Defence Staff was appointed to oversee the activities and growth of the armed forces as a whole. Inevitably, Oman began to look less to Britain and more to itself for its future security. A number of new units were formed and native Omanis groomed for command.

Among these were the 2,600-strong Sultan's Special Forces (SSF). Largely of Dhofari stock, and nicknamed the 'Lavender Hill Boys' in response to their gaudy berets, the SSF are SAS-trained, tough and aloof. They are also in many cases the sons of those who fought against the Sultan in the earlier Dhofari wars.